SH*T
TRUMP
SAYS

MAGA-nificent America-First Posts and Quotes
from our Bulletproof 45th and 47th President

THE
SEQUEL!

BLUEST☆NE
BOOKS

Bluestone Books
www.bluestonebooks.co

ISBN: 978-1-965636-26-8 (paper over board)
ISBN: 978-1-965636-27-5 (ebook)

Printed in India
10 9 8 7 6 5 4 3 2 1

Images used under license by Shutterstock.com

CONTENTS

SLOBS, THUGS, AND THE RADICAL LEFT

WE PLEDGE TO YOU THAT WE WILL ROOT OUT THE COMMUNISTS, MARXISTS, FASCISTS, AND THE RADICAL LEFT THUGS THAT LIVE LIKE VERMIN WITHIN THE CONFINES OF OUR COUNTRY.

Claremont, New Hampshire rally,
November 11, 2023

Thank you President Bukele, of El Salvador, for taking THE CRIMINALS THAT WERE SO STUPIDLY ALLOWED, BY THE CROOKED JOE BIDEN ADMINISTRATION, to enter our Country, and giving them such a wonderful place to live!

X, March 31, 2025

If Abe Lincoln came back to life, he would lose New York and he would lose California.

The Associated Press,
April 23, 2017

Crooked Hillary Clinton is the worst [and biggest] loser of all time. SHE JUST CAN'T STOP, which is so good for the Republican Party. HILLARY, GET ON WITH YOUR LIFE and give it another try in three years!

X, November 18, 2017

These Radical Left Lunatics are into the "Impeachment thing" again.

Truth Social,
May 2, 2025

Now if I don't get elected. . . It's going to be a bloodbath for the country.

Vandalia, Ohio rally,
March 16, 2024

I would have wiped the floor with the guys who weren't loyal, which I will now do. **I LOVE GETTING EVEN WITH PEOPLE.**

Charlie Rose,
November 6, 1992

If I happen to be president and I SEE SOMEBODY WHO'S DOING WELL AND BEATING ME VERY BADLY, I SAY GO DOWN AND INDICT THEM, mostly they would be out of business. They'd be out. They'd be out of the election.

Univision, November 9, 2023

She gets out and she starts asking me all sorts of ridiculous questions. You could see there was blood coming out of her eyes. **Blood coming out of her wherever.**

CNN, in reference to journalist Megyn Kelly, August 8, 2015

He's a *jealous fool* and not a bright person. He's good looking. Other than that, *he's got nothing.*

On Mitt Romney in an interview with
The New York Times, March 18, 2016

HOMEGROWNS ARE NEXT.

Oval Office appearance with
El Salvadoran President Bukele,
April 14, 2025

NOW [KAMALA HARRIS] WANTS TO DO TRANSGENDER OPERATIONS ON ILLEGAL ALIENS THAT ARE IN PRISON.

Harris-Trump Debate,
September 10, 2024

Kamala even wants to pass laws to outlaw RED MEAT to stop climate change. You know what that means? That means no more cows. . . . I guess eventually she's gonna mean no more people. Right? No more people.

Charlotte, North Carolina rally,
July 25, 2024

In Springfield, they're eating the dogs. The people that came in, they're eating the cats, they're eating, they are eating the pets of the people that live there.

Harris-Trump debate,
September 10, 2024

IF YOU CAN AVOID AN ALTERCATION, DO SO.

Trump: Think Like a Billionaire, 2004

If someone attacks you, do not hesitate. Go for the jugular.

Trump: Think Big, 2009

WE WILL IMMEDIATELY STOP ALL OF THE PILLAGING AND THEFT. VERY SIMPLY: IF YOU ROB A STORE, YOU CAN FULLY EXPECT TO BE SHOT AS YOU ARE LEAVING THAT STORE... SHOT! THE WORD THAT THEY SHOOT YOU WILL GET OUT WITHIN MINUTES AND OUR NATION, IN ONE DAY, WILL BE AN ENTIRELY DIFFERENT PLACE.

California Republican Party Convention,
September 29, 2023

THEY ARE THE MOST DISHONEST PEOPLE IN THE WORLD. THE MEDIA. THEY ARE THE WORST. THEY ARE THE WORST. THEY ARE VERY DISHONEST PEOPLE.

Indianapolis, Indiana rally
April 20, 2016

Crooked Joe Biden. I never called him that. I took the name away from Hillary Clinton. We call her beautiful Hillary now.

Pickens, South Carolina rally,
July 1, 2023

If I don't win the election, China will own the United States—you will have to learn to speak Chinese!

Conversation with Hugh Hewitt,
August 11, 2020

I am an innocent man being persecuted by some very bad, conflicted & corrupt people in a **WITCH HUNT THAT IS ILLEGAL** & should never have been allowed to start—And only because I won the Election! Despite this, great success!

X, March 3, 2019

DOJ just issued the McCabe report—which is a total disaster. He LIED! LIED! LIED! McCabe was totally controlled by Comey— McCabe is Comey!! No collusion, ALL MADE UP BY THIS DEN OF THIEVES AND LOWLIFES!

X, April 13, 2018

PRESIDENTIAL HARASSMENT!

X, April 18, 2019

SO, IT HAS NOW BEEN
DETERMINED, BY 18 PEOPLE
THAT TRULY HATE PRESIDENT
TRUMP, THAT THERE WAS NO
COLLUSION WITH RUSSIA.
IN FACT, IT WAS AN ILLEGAL
INVESTIGATION THAT SHOULD
NEVER HAVE BEEN ALLOWED
TO START. I FOUGHT BACK
HARD AGAINST THIS PHONY
& TREASONOUS HOAX!

X, April 10, 2019

I've known Jeff [Epstein] for fifteen years. Terrific guy. He's a lot of fun to be with. It is even said that he likes beautiful women as much as I do, and many of them are on the younger side. *No doubt about it—Jeffrey enjoys his social life.*

New York Magazine,
October 28, 2002

GOD, COUNTRY, AND KING TRUMP

I'D LIKE TO BE POPE. THAT WOULD BE MY NUMBER ONE CHOICE.

The White House, April 29, 2025

CONGESTION PRICING IS DEAD. Manhattan, and all of New York, is SAVED. LONG LIVE THE KING!

Truth Social, February 19, 2025

If CROOKED HILLARY would have won this election, and if she came here, which is about a zero percent chance after the election, SHE'D HAVE 200 PEOPLE IN A CONFERENCE ROOM IN A SMALL HOTEL.

Remarks about Hillary Clinton's
would-be crowd numbers,
Fargo, North Dakota, June 27, 2018

I DON'T PUT BORDERS ON MYSELF OR MY INTERESTS.

The Daily Mail,
October 30, 2010

And what happened is, **THEY RIGGED THE ELECTION, AND I BECAME PRESIDENT.** So that was a good thing, that was a good thing, that was quite an achievement for both of us. So I'll be president during the World Cup.

News conference with FIFA President
Gianni Infantino, March 8, 2025

I am your retribution.

Conservative Political
Action Conference,
March 4, 2023

Ted Cruz lifts the Bible high into the air and then LIES LIKE A DOG—over and over again! The Evangelicals in S.C. figured him out & said no!

X, February 23, 2016

I'M THE FATHER OF IVF.

Fox News town hall,
October 16, 2024

JUST A FEW MONTHS AGO, IN A BEAUTIFUL PENNSYLVANIA FIELD, AN ASSASSIN'S BULLET RIPPED THROUGH MY EAR. BUT I FELT THEN AND BELIEVE EVEN MORE SO NOW, THAT MY LIFE WAS SAVED FOR A REASON. I WAS SAVED BY GOD TO MAKE AMERICA GREAT AGAIN.

Inaugural Address,
January 20, 2025

Joe Biden got tongue-tied over the weekend when he was unable to properly deliver a very simple line about his decision to run for President. Get used to it, ANOTHER LOW I.Q. INDIVIDUAL!

X, March 18, 2019

After 50 years of failure, with nobody coming even close, I was able to kill Roe v. Wade, much to the "shock" of everyone.

Truth Social, May 17, 2023

When I drink my little wine—
which is about the only wine
I drink—and have my little
cracker, I guess that is a form
of asking for forgiveness,
and I do that as often as
possible because I feel cleansed.

CNN, July 18, 2015

IT'S AMAZING HOW OFTEN I AM RIGHT.

X, March 24, 2016

I was hundreds of millions in debt and beat bankruptcy twice—so what?

The Daily Mail,
October 30, 2010

WE LOVE THIS GUY. HE SAYS, **"YOU'RE NOT GOING TO BE A DICTATOR, ARE YOU?"** I SAID: "NO, NO, NO, **OTHER THAN DAY ONE.** WE'RE CLOSING THE BORDER, AND WE'RE DRILLING, DRILLING, DRILLING. AFTER THAT, I'M NOT A DICTATOR."

Commit to Caucus rally,
December 2, 2023

The question is: Do I do a chandelier? Beautiful crystal chandelier, top of the line, beautiful. Would be nice in here. It almost calls for it, but I don't know. We're more focused on China, Russia.

The Atlantic,
April 24, 2025

Something that had an effect on me was **when I saw the rocket ship** come back and get grabbed **like you grab a beautiful little baby.**

The Sean Hannity Show,
February 18, 2025

Very special. The kidney has a very special place in the heart. It's an incredible thing.

While signing an executive order,
July 10, 2019

And by the way, under the Trump administration you'll be saying "Merry Christmas" again when you go shopping, believe me. Merry Christmas. They've been downplaying that little beautiful phrase. You're going to be saying "Merry Christmas" again, folks.

Boy Scout Jamboree,
July 24, 2017

IT'S LIBERATION DAY IN AMERICA!

Truth Social, April 2, 2025

THE OPERATION IS OVER!
THE PATIENT LIVED,
AND IS HEALING. THE
PROGNOSIS IS THAT THE
PATIENT WILL BE FAR
STRONGER, BIGGER,
BETTER, AND MORE
RESILIENT THAN EVER
BEFORE. MAKE AMERICA
GREAT AGAIN!!!

Truth Social, April 3, 2025

I have stopped
all government
censorship and
BROUGHT BACK
FREE SPEECH in
America. It's back.

Joint Session Address to Congress,
March 4, 2025

IF YOU'RE THE PRESIDENT OF
THE UNITED STATES, YOU CAN
DECLASSIFY JUST BY SAYING IT'S
DECLASSIFIED, EVEN BY THINKING
ABOUT IT, BECAUSE YOU'RE SENDING
IT TO MAR-A-LAGO OR TO
WHEREVER YOU'RE SENDING IT.
AND THERE DOESN'T HAVE TO BE A
PROCESS. THERE CAN BE A PROCESS,
BUT THERE DOESN'T HAVE TO BE.

Fox News,
September 21, 2022

Nobody has done
more for Christianity
or for evangelicals—
or for religion itself—
than I have.

Flashpoint, September 30, 2021

REPUBLICAN LEADERSHIP ONLY WANTS THE PATH OF LEAST RESISTANCE. OUR LEADERS (NOT ME, OF COURSE!) ARE PATHETIC.

X, December 29, 2020

I did something good: I made
Juneteenth very famous. It's
actually an important event,
an important time. But
nobody had ever heard of it.

Oval Office,
June 17, 2020

My primary consultant is myself .

Morning Joe, MSNBC,
March 16, 2016

WINNERS WHO ALWAYS WIN

THE USA HAS A LOT OF WINNING TO DO! DJT

X, January 27, 2025

Don't be Weak!
Don't be Stupid!
Don't be a PANICAN
(A new party based
on Weak and
Stupid people!).

X, April 7, 2025

THE BEST DEFINITION OF INTELLIGENCE IS THE ABILITY TO PREDICT THE FUTURE!!!

Truth Social, April 14, 2025

[ELON MUSK] KNOWS THOSE COMPUTERS BETTER THAN ANYBODY. ALL THOSE COMPUTERS. THOSE VOTE-COUNTING COMPUTERS. AND WE ENDED UP WINNING PENNSYLVANIA LIKE IN A LANDSLIDE.

Washington D.C. victory rally,
January 19, 2025

NOBODY CAN DRAW CROWDS LIKE ME... I'M THE GREATEST OF ALL TIME. MAYBE GREATER EVEN THAN ELVIS. ELVIS HAD A GUITAR, I DON'T HAVE A GUITAR. I DON'T HAVE THE PRIVILEGE OF A GUITAR.

Uniondale, New York rally,
September 18, 2024

[The Continental Army] manned the air, it rammed the ramparts, it took over the airports, it did everything it had to do, and at Fort McHenry, under the rockets' red glare, it had nothing but victory.

July 4th speech, 2019

I'm a bit of a
P. T. Barnum.
I make stars
out of everyone.

The Observer, July 7, 1991

I LOVE WHAT HE SAID, LIKE THREE "SUPER BOWLS A DAY FOR A MONTH." THAT'S WHAT IT IS. THAT'S REALLY AMAZING WHEN YOU THINK OF IT. I'VE NEVER HEARD THAT EXPRESSION. THAT'S A LOT.

News conference with FIFA President
Gianni Infantino, March 7, 2025

Even if you vote [for me] and then pass away, it's worth it.

Indianola, Iowa rally,
January 14, 2024

Republicans: We are doing **GREAT.** Stay on Line. Do not let them move you. **STAY ON LINE AND VOTE!**

X, November 5, 2024

I **WIN**, I ALWAYS **WIN**. IN THE END **I ALWAYS WIN**, WHETHER IT'S IN GOLF, WHETHER IT'S IN TENNIS, WHETHER IT'S IN LIFE, **I JUST ALWAYS WIN**. AND I TELL PEOPLE **I ALWAYS WIN**, BECAUSE I DO.

TrumpNation:
The Art of Being The Donald,
2005

I would give myself an A+.

Fox & Friends,
April 27, 2018

We are going to conquer the vast frontiers of science, and we are going to lead humanity into space and PLANT THE AMERICAN FLAG ON THE PLANET MARS, AND EVEN FAR BEYOND.

Joint Session Address to Congress,
March 4, 2025

We are going to be very kind. . . . Somebody said that about me the other day, who doesn't know me very well. **They said— "You are such a kind person"** *and I said, "Say that again." They said, "You are a kind person."* **I said, "I've never heard that before."**

CNN, April 1, 2025

Well, there are plans. . . there are—not plans— *there are methods—there* *are methods which you* *could [get a third term].* *. . . A lot of people want* *me to do it. . . . I'm not* *joking. I'm not joking.*

NBC News,
March 30, 2025

In fact, it has been stated by many that the first month of our presidency—it's our presidency—is the most successful in the history of our nation. And what makes it even more impressive is that, do you know [who] No. 2 is? George Washington. How about that? I don't know about that list. But we'll take it.

Joint Session Address to Congress,
March 4, 2025

And I'll get the war with Ukraine and Russia ended. If I'm President-Elect, **I'll get it done before even becoming president.**

Harris-Trump Debate,
September 10, 2024

[The debate] was 3 on 1, but they were mentally challenged people, against one person of extraordinary genius.

Truth Social,
September 14, 2024

If any senior doesn't vote for Trump, we're gonna have to send you to a psychiatrist to have your head examined.

Mint Hill, North Carolina speech,
September 25, 2024

But just to finish, **I got more votes than any Republican in history by far.** In fact, I got more votes than any president, sitting president in history by far.

Harris-Trump Debate,
September 10, 2024

I think I've been a very good husband.

CNN, February 9, 2011

What the hell do I know, I've been divorced twice?

Trump: Think Big, 2007

Many say I am the greatest star-maker of all time. BUT SOME OF THE STARS I PRODUCED ARE ACTUALLY MADE OF GARBAGE.

Save America newsletter,
July 15, 2021

Well, I think if [the GOP candidates] win, I SHOULD GET ALL THE CREDIT. AND IF THEY LOSE, I SHOULD NOT BE BLAMED AT ALL, OK, but it'll probably be just the opposite.

NewsNation,
November 8, 2022

[Coronavirus is] going to disappear. One day it's like a miracle, it will disappear. And from our shores, we— you know, it could get worse before it gets better. It could maybe go away. We'll see what happens. Nobody really knows.

White House African American History Month reception, February 27, 2020

ORATORICAL GENIUS

I have a very
good brain
**AND I'VE
SAID A
LOT OF
THINGS.**

Morning Joe, MSNBC,
March 16, 2016

You know, I do the weave.

You know what the weave is?

**I'LL TALK ABOUT
LIKE NINE DIFFERENT
THINGS, AND THEY
ALL COME BACK
BRILLIANTLY TOGETHER,**
and it's like, friends of mine that
are, like, English professors, they
say, "It's the most brilliant thing
I've ever seen."

Johnstown, Pennsylvania rally,
August 30, 2024

I have a plan to visit, not the site. Because you tell me, what's the site? The water? You want me to go swimming?

Remarks on Washington D.C. plane crash, January 30, 2025

[Suppose] you brought the light inside of the body, which you could do either through the skin or in some other way. . . . The whole concept of the light, the way it kills [the coronavirus] in one minute. That's, uh, that's pretty powerful.

White House Coronavirus Task Force Briefing, April 23, 2020

I'm totally pro-choice.

Fox News,
October 31, 1999

I'm pro-life.

Conservative Political
Action Conference,
February 10, 2011

The reason my hair looks so neat all the time is because I don't have to deal with the elements. I live in the building where I work. I take an elevator from my bedroom to my office. The rest of the time, I'm either in my stretch limousine, my private jet, my helicopter, or my private club in Palm Beach Florida.

Trump: How to Get Rich, 2004

I DIDN'T HAVE SEX WITH A PORN STAR, NUMBER ONE.

Biden-Trump debate,
June 27, 2024

I [write posts] quickly as hell. **You'd be amazed.** You'd be impressed. **And I like doing them myself.** Sometimes I dictate them out, but I like doing them myself.

The Atlantic, April 24, 2025

I spoke to over
100 countries.
**YOU WOULDN'T
BELIEVE HOW
MANY COUNTRIES
THERE ARE.**

Mar-a-Lago Press Conference,
December 16, 2024

THIS IS A TOUGH HURRICANE, ONE OF THE WETTEST WE'VE EVER SEEN FROM THE STANDPOINT OF WATER.

The White House,
September 19, 2018

Trump Tower, like a good friend, was there when I needed it.

The Art of the Comeback, 1997

I read where [Kamala Harris] was not Black. . . and then I read that she was Black, and that's OK. Either one was OK with me. That's up to her.

Harris-Trump debate,
September 10, 2024

IF WE GO WITH KAMALA, YOU WON'T HAVE ANY COWS ANYMORE. THEY WANT TO DO THINGS LIKE NO MORE COWS AND NO WINDOWS IN BUILDINGS.

Fox & Friends,
October 18, 2024

OUR K-9, AS THEY CALL— I CALL IT A DOG, A BEAUTIFUL DOG, A TALENTED DOG.

Remarks on death of ISIS leader,
October 27, 2019

You know bullies? You know what a bully is, right? *You know the bully, I've always—and I found it throughout my life—a bully is the weakest person.*

Speaking to reporters,
February 12, 2025

I could've been anywhere I wanted to be. I could've had those waves smacking me in the face. **That white, beautiful white skin that I have would be nice and tan. I got the whitest skin 'cause I never have time to go out in the sun.** But I have that beautiful white, and you know what? It could've been beautiful, tanned, beautiful.

Warren, Michigan rally,
November 2, 2024

Let's not do any more questions. Let's just listen to music. Let's make it into a music. Who the hell wants to hear questions, right?

Oaks, Pennsylvania town hall,
October 14, 2024

[Tim Walz] also says execution after birth, it's execution, no longer abortion, because the baby is born, is okay. And that's not okay with me.

Harris-Trump Debate,
September 10, 2024

I'm cognitively very strong.

Indiana, Pennsylvania rally,
September 23, 2024

Nobody's ever called me weird. I'm a lot of things, but weird I'm not. **You notice the evening news, every one of them, you know, they introduced the word "weird," and all of a sudden they're talking about "weird."** No, we're not weird people. We're actually just the opposite. We're right down the middle. No, we're not weird. We're very solid people.

Bozeman, Montana rally,
August 1, 2024

You know what I'd do if there was a shark or you get electrocuted? I'll take electrocution every single time. I'm not getting near the shark!

Las Vegas, Nevada rally,
June 10, 2024

It's always good to do things nice and complicated so that nobody can figure it out.

The New Yorker,
May 19, 1997

The simplest approach is often the most effective.

Trump: The Art of the Deal, 1987

THEY WANT TO GO AFTER ME BECAUSE I HAVE, THEY THINK, A BIG MOUTH. I DON'T HAVE A BIG MOUTH, YOU KNOW WHAT I HAVE, I HAVE A MOUTH THAT TELLS THE TRUTH.

Perry, Georgia rally,
September 25, 2021

I tested positively toward negative, right? So, no, I tested perfectly this morning, meaning— meaning I tested negative. . . . **BUT THAT'S A WAY OF SAYING IT: POSITIVELY TOWARD THE NEGATIVE.**

The White House,
May 21, 2020

It's called "social media." It's social media. It gets out. I have, you know, hundreds of millions of people. Number one on Facebook. Did you know I was number one on Facebook? I mean, I just found out I'm number one on Facebook. I thought that was very nice for whatever it means. No, it represents something.

Coronavirus task force meeting,
April 1, 2020

GREETINGS, SALUTATIONS, AND EXECUTIVE ORDERS

Vladimir, STOP!

Truth Social,
April 24, 2025

I have concepts of a plan.

Harris-Trump debate,
September 10, 2024

You write a beautiful executive—and you sign it and you assume it's going to be done, but it's not. What he does is he takes it, and with his hundred geniuses—he's got some very brilliant young people working for him that dress much worse than him, actually.

The Sean Hannity Show,
February 1, 2025

As the New Year fast approaches, I would like to wish an early New Year's salutation to crooked Joe Biden and his group of radical left misfits and thugs on their never-ending attempt to destroy our nation through lawfare, invasion and rigging elections.

Truth Social, December 31, 2023

TRUMP WAS RIGHT ABOUT EVERYTHING!

X, January 3, 2025

Big press conference today at Four Seasons Total Landscaping— 11:30am!

X, November 7, 2020

I loved my previous life. I had so many things going. **This is more work than in my previous life.** I thought it would be easier.

Reuters, April 27, 2017

THESE PEOPLE. WE GOT A BUNCHA REAL DUMMIES, I'LL TELL YA.

The Washington Post,
January 21, 2016

The late, great Hannibal Lecter is a wonderful man. He oftentimes would have a friend for dinner. Remember the last scene? "Excuse me. I'm about to have a friend for dinner," as this poor doctor walked by. "I'm about to have a friend for dinner." But Hannibal Lecter. Congratulations. The late, great Hannibal Lecter.

Wildwood, New Jersey rally,
May 11, 2024

I want you to remember what they did to me. They tortured me in the Fulton County Jail, and **TOOK MY MUGSHOT.** So guess what? I put it on a mug for the **WHOLE WORLD TO SEE!**

Trump fundraising email, June 24, 2024

If you took a poll in the FBI, **I WOULD WIN THAT POLL** more than anyone has ever won a poll.

Fox & Friends,
June 15, 2018

[Kim Jong-un] speaks and his people sit up at attention. **I WANT** my people to do the same.

Fox & Friends,
June 15, 2018

I'm really rich.

2016 presidential
campaign announcement,
New York, June 16, 2015

I THINK WE'VE DONE MORE THAN PERHAPS ANY PRESIDENT IN THE FIRST 100 DAYS.

The Washington Examiner,
April 28, 2017

MICHAEL SCHERER:
I got a call from your cellphone number at 1:30 a.m.

DONALD TRUMP:
Really? Oh, no, that's another—that sounds like another Signal thing.

The Atlantic, April 24, 2025

In my case, I like to take a nice shower, take care of my beautiful hair. . . . I have to stand under the shower for 15 minutes until it gets wet. It comes out drip, drip, drip. It's ridiculous.

While signing an executive order,
April 10, 2025

I look very much
forward to showing
my financials,
because they are
HUGE.

Time, April 11, 2011

It's really cold outside, they are calling it a major freeze, weeks ahead of normal.

MAN, WE COULD USE A BIG FAT DOSE OF GLOBAL WARMING!

X, October 19, 2015

Millions and millions of women—cervical cancer, breast cancer—are helped by Planned Parenthood. So you can say whatever you want, but they have millions of women going through Planned Parenthood that are helped greatly.

Republican presidential debate in Houston, Texas, February 25, 2016

But Planned Parenthood should absolutely be defunded. I mean, if you look at what's going on with that, it's terrible.

Fox News Sunday,
October 18, 2015

BUT YOU ALSO HAD PEOPLE THAT WERE VERY FINE PEOPLE ON BOTH SIDES.

To a reporter in reference to
the participants of the deadly
Charlottesville, Virginia protest,
August 15, 2017

*I will be phenomenal
to the women. I mean,
I want to help women.*

Face the Nation,
August 9, 2015

I'm an environmentalist.

Larry King Live, CNN,
April 28, 2010

Global warming is a total, and very expensive, hoax!

X, December 6, 2013

I would like to extend my best wishes to all, **even the haters and losers,** on this special date, September 11th.

X, September 11, 2013

Happy Easter to all **including the Radical Left Maniacs** who are trying everything to destroy our country May they not succeed, but let them, nevertheless, be happy, healthy, wealthy and well!

Save America newsletter,
April 17, 2022

I'M
FUCKED.

In response to the appointment of Special Counsel for the Russia investigation, Mueller Report, March 17, 2017

D.E.I.,
DOUBTERS,
AND
DEPORTATIONS

THANK YOU PRESIDENT
BUKELE, OF EL SALVADOR,
FOR TAKING THE
CRIMINALS THAT WERE
SO STUPIDLY ALLOWED,
BY THE CROOKED JOE
BIDEN ADMINISTRATION,
TO ENTER OUR COUNTRY,
AND GIVING THEM SUCH
A WONDERFUL PLACE
TO LIVE!

X, March 31, 2025

I will never change this hairstyle, I like it. It fits my head. Those who criticize me are only losers and envy people. And it is not a wig, it's my hair. **Do you want to touch it?**

Veja, February 18, 2014

It's like in golf... A lot of people—
I don't want this to sound trivial—
but a lot of people are switching
to these really long putters, very
unattractive... **IT'S WEIRD.** You see
these great players with these really
long putters, because they can't sink
three-footers anymore. And **I HATE IT.**
I am a traditionalist. I have so many
fabulous friends who happen to
be gay, but I am a traditionalist.

The New York Times,
regarding his stance on gay marriage,
May 1, 2011

AFTER HAVING WRITTEN MANY
BEST-SELLING BOOKS, AND
SOMEWHAT PRIDING MYSELF ON
MY ABILITY TO WRITE, IT SHOULD
BE NOTED THAT THE FAKE NEWS
CONSTANTLY LIKES TO PORE OVER
MY TWEETS LOOKING FOR A
MISTAKE. I CAPITALIZE CERTAIN
WORDS ONLY FOR EMPHASIS,
NOT B/C THEY SHOULD BE
CAPITALIZED!

X, July 3, 2018

We've ended the tyranny of so-called diversity, equity and inclusion policies all across the entire federal government and indeed the private sector and our military. And our country will be "woke" no longer.

Joint Session Address to Congress,
March 4, 2025

Will someone from his depleted and food-starved regime please inform him that I too have a Nuclear Button, but it is a much bigger & more powerful one than his, and my Button works!

X, in reference to
Supreme Leader of North Korea
Kim Jong-un's nuclear weapons,
January 2, 2018

There's nothing that's not a threat. But sometimes, you have to fight three of these threats. You know, you can't just—like Google. I'm not a fan of Google. They treat me badly. . . . We have to straighten out our press.

Bloomberg News,
October 13, 2024

They've released the genie out of the box.

Univision, November 9, 2023

I have great friends. Wayne Gretzky's a friend of mine. I mean, I have great friends. I said to Wayne, "I'm gonna give you a pass, Wayne." I don't want to ruin his reputation in Canada. I said, "Just pretend you don't know me."

The Atlantic, April 24, 2025

Uh, Obamagate. It's been going on for a long time. It's been going on from before I even got elected, and it's a disgrace that it happened, and if you look at what's gone on and if you look at now all of this information that's being released, and from what I understand that's only the beginning. Some terrible things happened and it should never be allowed to happen in our country again, and you'll be seeing what's going on over the coming weeks.

The Washington Post press conference,
May 11, 2020

WE'RE ROUNDING 'EM UP
IN A VERY HUMANE WAY,
IN A VERY NICE WAY.
AND THEY'RE GOING TO BE
HAPPY BECAUSE THEY
WANT TO BE LEGALIZED.
AND, BY THE WAY, I KNOW
IT DOESN'T SOUND NICE.
BUT NOT EVERYTHING
IS NICE.

60 Minutes,
September 27, 2015

THE DEMOCRATS ARE
TRYING TO BELITTLE
THE CONCEPT OF A
WALL, CALLING IT OLD
FASHIONED. THE FACT
IS THERE IS NOTHING
ELSE'S THAT WILL WORK,
AND THAT HAS BEEN
TRUE FOR THOUSANDS
OF YEARS. IT'S LIKE
THE WHEEL, THERE IS
NOTHING BETTER. I KNOW
TECH BETTER THAN
ANYONE, & TECHNOLOGY...

X, December 21, 2018

YOU'RE DISGUSTING.

To opposing counsel upon her request for a
breast-pump break during court proceedings,
The New York Times, July 28, 2015

I think the bigger problem is the enemy from within, not even the people that have come in and [are] destroying our country. . . . **We have some very bad people. We have some sick people.**

Sunday Morning Futures,
October 13, 2024

**Stay as close
to home
as possible.
Travel is
time-consuming
and, in my
opinion, boring.**

Trump: Surviving at the Top, 1990

There's no excuse
for staying home;
the world's
too fantastic
to miss out on it.
I wish I could
travel more.

*Trump: Think Like a
Billionaire, 2004*

I AM PROUD TO SHUT DOWN THE GOVERNMENT FOR BORDER SECURITY.

Oval Office meeting with Chuck Schumer and Nancy Pelosi prior to the longest and most damaging government shutdown in United States history, December 11, 2018

Why are we having
all these people from
shithole countries
coming here?

The White House,
January 11, 2018

When you see the other side chopping off heads, waterboarding doesn't sound very severe.

Interview with
ABC's Jonathan Karl,
August 2, 2016

I think I could have stopped it because I have very tough illegal immigration policies, and people aren't coming into this country unless they're vetted and vetted properly.

On preventing the September 11th terrorist attacks in an interview with *Hannity*, October 20, 2015

Eminent domain is wonderful.

Fox News,
October 6, 2015

Wokeness is trouble. Wokeness is bad. It's gone. And we feel so much better for it, don't we?

Joint Session Address to Congress,
March 4, 2025

I have been investigated more than any person in the history of the United States of America...

Truth Social, May 4, 2025

TARIFFS, TESLA, AND A BEAUTIFUL ECONOMY

EVERYTHING IS COMPUTER!

White House car show,
March 11, 2025

We are doing really well on our TARIFF POLICY. Very exciting for America, and the World!!! It is moving along quickly. DJT

Truth Social, April 11, 2025

YOU TAKE A LOOK AT BACON AND SOME OF THESE PRODUCTS AND SOME PEOPLE DON'T EAT BACON ANY MORE. WE ARE GOING TO GET THE ENERGY PRICES DOWN. WHEN WE GET ENERGY DOWN—YOU KNOW, THIS WAS CAUSED BY THEIR HORRIBLE ENERGY— WIND, THEY WANT WIND ALL OVER THE PLACE. BUT WHEN IT DOESN'T BLOW, WE HAVE A LITTLE PROBLEM.

La Crosse, Wisconsin rally,
August 30, 2024

I say it would make a great 51st state. I love other nations. I love Canada.

The Atlantic, April 28, 2025

I am the world's greatest person.

Phone conversation with Australian
Prime Minister Malcolm Turnbull,
January 28, 2017

When a country (USA) is losing many billions of dollars on trade with virtually every country it does business with, trade wars are good, and easy to win. Example, when we are down $100 billion with a certain country and they get cute, don't trade anymore—we win big. It's easy!

X, March 2, 2018

I'm telling you, **THESE COUNTRIES ARE CALLING US UP KISSING MY ASS.** They are dying to make a deal. "Please, please, sir, make a deal. I'll do anything. I'll do anything, sir."

National Republican Congressional
Committee Dinner, April 8, 2025

It was a pleasure to have dinner the other night with Governor Justin Trudeau of the Great State of Canada

Truth Social, December 9, 2024

For all of the money we are spending, NASA should NOT be talking about going to the Moon—We did that 50 years ago. They should be focused on the much bigger things we are doing, including Mars (of which the Moon is a part), Defense and Science!

X, June 7, 2019

For decades, our country has been looted, pillaged, raped and plundered by nations near and far, both friend and foe alike.

Liberation Day speech,
April 2, 2025

I AM A TARIFF MAN. When people or countries come in to raid the great wealth of our Nation, I want them to pay for the privilege of doing so. It will always be the best way to max out our economic power. We are right now taking in $billions in Tariffs. MAKE AMERICA RICH AGAIN

X, December 4, 2018

The Wall is being built and is well under construction. Big impact will be made. Many additional contracts are close to being signed. Far ahead of schedule despite all of the Democrat Obstruction and Fake News!

X, March 8, 2019

Big business is not worried about the Tariffs, because they know they are here to stay, but they are focused on the **BIG, BEAUTIFUL DEAL,** which will **SUPERCHARGE** our Economy. Very important. Going on right now!!!

Truth Social, April 5, 2025

It's such an old-fashioned term but a beautiful term: groceries. It sort of says a bag with different things in it.

Liberation Day speech,
April 2, 2025

TO THE MANY INVESTORS COMING INTO THE UNITED STATES AND INVESTING MASSIVE AMOUNTS OF MONEY, MY POLICIES WILL NEVER CHANGE. THIS IS A GREAT TIME TO GET RICH, RICHER THAN EVER BEFORE!!!

Truth Social, April 5, 2025

THIS IS A GREAT TIME TO BUY.

Truth Social, April 9, 2025

Republicans, it is more important now, than ever, that we pass THE ONE, BIG, BEAUTIFUL BILL. The USA will Soar like never before!!!

Truth Social, April 9, 2025

And I'm very proud of it because you are very, very special people. That I can tell you. Thank you. NICE HAT. LOOK AT THAT BEAUTIFUL HAT.

Roundtable discussion on Tax Reform, White Sulphur Springs, West Virginia, April 5, 2018

I turn off [Barron's] laptop, I said, "Oh good," and I go back five minutes later, he's got his laptop. I said, "How'd you do that?" "None of your business, Dad." He's got an unbelievable aptitude in technology.

Fox News,
March 20, 2025

I LOVE TESLER!

White House car show,
March 11, 2025

This is one of the most important days, in my opinion, in American history.

Rose Garden tariff announcement,
April 2, 2025

To me, **THE MOST BEAUTIFUL WORD IN THE DICTIONARY IS TARIFF**, and it's my favorite word. It needs a public relations firm.

Bloomberg News,
October 15, 2024

I've made a lot of money with China, but you know what, they know. They told me. That's how they do it. It's the single greatest tool they have, currency manipulation, and they're grand masters. They do a great job. I congratulate them. I'm not angry at China. I'm angry at our country for allowing them to do it.

St. Augustine, Florida rally
October 24, 2016

Why would I call China a currency manipulator when they are working with us on the North Korean problem? We will see what happens!

X, April 16, 2017

You hear lots of people say that a great deal is when both sides win. That is a bunch of crap.

Trump: Think Big, 2007

BE COOL!
Everything is going to work out well. The USA will be bigger and better than ever before!

Truth Social, April 9, 2025

I'm for electric cars. I have to be, you know, because Elon endorsed me very strongly. So I have no choice.

Atlanta, Georgia rally,
August 5, 2024